NFT Digital Dynasty

Sean Mike Kelly

Published by Avinash Walton, 2025.

While every precaution has been taken in the preparation of this book, the publisher assumes no responsibility for errors or omissions, or for damages resulting from the use of the information contained herein.

NFT DIGITAL DYNASTY

First edition. June 26, 2025.

ISBN: 979-8231091065

Written by Sean Mike Kelly.

Table of Contents

Chapter 1: The NFT Revolution

In every generation, there's a shift—a moment when technology flips the rules of the game. For our generation, that moment came with **NFTs**.

NFTs, or *Non-Fungible Tokens*, aren't just digital art. They're proof of ownership in a world that's rapidly digitizing everything. From how we shop to how we collect, invest, and engage—NFTs changed the landscape forever.

When I first heard about NFTs, I didn't jump in immediately. I had already built **Jersey Champs**, scaled e-commerce brands, and hosted top-tier entrepreneurs on my podcast *Digital Social Hour*. But something about NFTs felt...different.

And then came **Chibi Dinos**—my first major NFT project. It wasn't just about launching cool-looking avatars; it was about **building community**, **creating digital assets**, and giving value that lasted beyond the hype.

What Are NFTs, Really?

MOST PEOPLE DEFINE NFTs as "digital collectibles." That's only scratching the surface. NFTs are:

- **Smart contracts** built on blockchain
- **Unique tokens** that can't be replicated

- **Digital ownership receipts** (proving you own something on the internet)

If a regular crypto coin like Bitcoin is fungible (1 BTC = 1 BTC), an NFT is **non-fungible**—each one is one-of-a-kind. Think digital baseball cards. But also think: concert tickets, event passes, art licenses, exclusive memberships.

Why NFTs Matter in Business

LET'S GET REAL. NFTS are more than hype—they're tools. Businesses (mine included) have used NFTs to:

- **Reward loyalty** (imagine a brand giving lifetime discounts through an NFT)
- **Create exclusivity** (access to events, merch, or communities)
- **Build ecosystems** (like games, DAO communities, and tokenized assets)
- **Raise capital** (launch an NFT collection = fund your startup)

When we launched Chibi Dinos, we weren't just making artwork—we were creating a **Web3 sports franchise**. We built a lore, a game plan, a fanbase. The NFTs were just the entry point.

Web2 vs Web3: The Mindset Shift

THE TRADITIONAL INTERNET (Web2) is controlled by platforms—Facebook, YouTube, Shopify. You create content, but they own the audience.

In Web3? **Ownership flips to the user.** NFTs are the gateway to this new ownership economy.

As an entrepreneur, this is the **biggest opportunity** we've ever seen to:

- Cut out the middleman
- Build direct-to-fan brands
- Tokenize value in real time

Why I Wrote This Book

THERE'S TOO MUCH NOISE in the NFT space. Scams. Hype. Confusion.

But I've been through it. I've seen what works. And I've helped creators and entrepreneurs use NFTs the *right way*—as tools for building real value.

This book is for:

- Hustlers ready to build in Web3
- Creators who want more than likes
- Entrepreneurs who see the next wave coming

I won't just teach you *what* NFTs are—I'll show you *how* to use them to build your own **digital empire**.

> *The future of ownership is digital. The future of branding is community. The future of business is blockchain.*
>
> — *Sean Mike Kelly*

Chapter 2: From JPEGs to Empires

NFTs That Actually Matter

When the world first caught wind of NFTs, headlines screamed million-dollar sales of pixelated apes and cats. For most people, NFTs became a punchline—"just overpriced JPEGs." And yeah, the memes were hilarious. But here's the truth:

JPEGs don't change the world. Business models do.

If you're reading this, I know you're not here for hype. You're here to **build something real**. I was too. That's why I didn't stop at digital art drops—I saw NFTs as a bridge to something bigger:

Ownership. Loyalty. Culture. Community. Legacy.

Let's break it down.

The Problem: Digital Doesn't Equal Ownership

BEFORE NFTS, YOUR ONLINE purchases—songs, eBooks, digital goods—weren't really *yours*. You had access, sure. But Apple, Amazon, or Instagram could pull the plug anytime. You don't own your followers. You don't own your skins. You don't even own that music you "bought" on iTunes.

NFTs changed that.

With NFTs, ownership is **decentralized**, **verifiable**, and **resellable**. You buy it, you own it. No third-party permission needed.

Real-World Utility: NFTs with Purpose

LET ME SHOW YOU HOW smart people are using NFTs to **build empires**, not just sell art:

1. Event Access

NFTS AS DIGITAL TICKETS. Burn it to get in. Hold it to unlock future events. Some music artists are giving **VIP lifetime access** through NFTs.

2. Brand Loyalty

IMAGINE STARBUCKS GIVING you an NFT that earns points, offers early menu drops, or discounts. Sounds futuristic? They're doing it. It's called **Odyssey**.

3. Career & Network Passes

ENTREPRENEURS ARE LAUNCHING NFT-gated communities with job boards, live calls, and investment deals. Instead of paying monthly, you buy the NFT once and hold.

4. Fashion & Merch

NFTS ARE NOW TIED TO physical goods. Buy a hoodie NFT? You can redeem it for a real hoodie—plus, the NFT proves you were part of a limited drop.

5. Gaming & Digital Land

NFTS INSIDE GAMES LET players own land, weapons, and skins—and trade them for real value. You don't just play—you invest and earn.

Sean's Take: The Chibi Dinos Case Study

WHEN I LAUNCHED **Chibi Dinos**, I didn't just want another PFP (*profile picture*) project. I wanted a full-blown **digital franchise**:

- NBA-style teams
- Lore and storytelling
- In-game rewards
- Brand partnerships
- Utility-packed NFTs that live in games, merch, and events

What we created wasn't a "drop"—it was a **launchpad**. That's how you build an NFT empire.

Blueprint for a Meaningful NFT Project

IF YOU'RE PLANNING to build your own NFT project, here's what you need:

A strong narrative: Why does it exist? What's the mission?
Clear utility: What can holders *do* with it?
Community-first mindset: Engage, listen, evolve.
Ongoing value: Make holders proud long after the mint.

A real brand: Design. Voice. Vision. Feel. Treat it like a business.

This is the difference between a pump-and-dump and a project that stands the test of time.

Common Mistakes New Creators Make

LAUNCHING WITHOUT UTILITY

Copy-paste art with no story

Chasing floor prices instead of brand building

Ignoring community feedback

Relying only on influencers for hype

Hype fades. Vision stays.

It's not about NFTs. It's about what you build with them.

— Sean Mike Kelly

Chapter 3: The Launch

Creating Your First NFT Project

So, you've got the vision. You've understood the value. And now you're ready to step into the arena.

Launching an NFT project isn't just about minting a few thousand images and hoping they sell out overnight. That's **2019 energy**. Today's market demands **clarity**, **community**, and **carefully crafted experiences.**

The good news? With the right steps, you can **stand out**, create long-term value, and build your own digital legacy.

This chapter is your **end-to-end launch blueprint.**

Step 1: Define Your Purpose

BEFORE YOU EVEN TOUCH a blockchain, answer these questions:

- Why are you launching this NFT?
- Who is it for?
- What value does it offer beyond the image?
- How will it evolve over time?

If your answer is just "to make money," stop here. The market can smell inauthenticity. Real projects **solve a problem or create real culture.**

Step 2: Create the Artwork or Asset

YOU DON'T NEED TO BE an artist—but your NFTs should:

- Reflect a **distinct brand identity**
- Be either **1/1 artworks**, **generative collections**, or **utility tokens**
- Be optimized in size (e.g., under 1MB for speed and blockchain cost)
- Use **layers and traits** for generative projects (like hats, glasses, backgrounds, etc.)

Tool tips:

- Adobe Illustrator / Photoshop for custom art
- Figma for UI assets
- NFT-Inator or Bueno for trait-based generation

Step 3: Choose Your Blockchain

EACH CHAIN HAS PROS and cons:

Blockchain	Pros	Cons
Ethereum	Popular, strong community	High gas fees
Polygon	Cheap, eco-friendly	Less prestige
Solana	Fast, low cost	Still growing
Flow	Used by NBA Top Shot	Smaller dev community

For most new creators, **Polygon** is a solid starting point.

Step 4: Smart Contract Setup

YOU NEED A SMART CONTRACT to:

- Define ownership
- Handle royalties
- Enable transfers, burns, staking, etc.

You can use:

- **Manifold.xyz** (great for creators, easy UI)
- **Thirdweb.com** (low-code, dev-friendly)
- **Hardhat/Remix** (if you have Solidity devs)

Always **test on testnet first** (like Rinkeby or Mumbai)!

Step 5: Build the Minting Website

YOUR MINTING SITE IS where users mint NFTs directly. Essentials include:

- Countdown timer
- Project story / roadmap
- Team section
- FAQs
- Wallet connect (MetaMask, WalletConnect)
- Mint button (linked to your contract)

Pro tip: Use tools like **Thirdweb**, **Moralis**, or **Alchemy** to simplify Web3 integration.

Step 6: Marketing & Community Building

START **90 days before** launch.

Pre-Launch Strategy:

- Tease the project with visuals and lore
- Launch a **Discord or Telegram**
- Post consistent updates on Twitter
- Engage with NFT communities and cross-collab
- Share **behind-the-scenes** of the art/dev journey

Influencer Hype?

YES, BUT ONLY IF:

- They *actually engage*
- They align with your project's values
- You use them to build—not fake demand

Step 7: Set Mint Price & Supply

COMMON MODELS:

- 10,000 supply @ 0.05 ETH
- Limited drop (100–500) @ higher price
- Free mint, royalties on resale

Think like a startup:
What price balances accessibility with long-term funding?

Step 8: Launch Day Checklist

SMART CONTRACT VERIFIED

Website tested

Community warmed up

Mods and devs on standby

Wallets ready for mint

Social media queued

Optional: Do a **stealth mint** for early insiders or whitelist phase.

Step 9: Post-Launch Plan

AFTER MINT IS WHERE the real game starts:

- Keep the community updated
- Airdrop perks or new content
- Build or launch promised utilities
- Track secondary market activity
- NEVER go silent!

Projects die when founders disappear. Projects thrive when **owners show up every day**.

> *NFTs aren't the product. They're the pass. Your experience is what builds the empire.*
>
> *— Sean Mike Kelly*

Chapter 4: Monetization & Revenue Models in NFTs

From Drops to Dollars

Let's face it—building something meaningful in Web3 isn't just about art, hype, or community buzz.

It's also about **sustainability**.

You can have a jaw-dropping mint day. But if your project doesn't bring in consistent revenue or offer long-term value, it'll fizzle out like most PFP collections did post-2021.

As someone who's built businesses that didn't just "launch"—they *lasted*—I'm here to break down how you can turn your NFT idea into a **money-making machine** while staying true to your community and mission.

Revenue Stream #1: Primary Sales (The Mint)

THIS IS THE STARTING line for most NFT projects.

What it is:

Selling NFTs during the initial launch or pre-sale to your community, whitelisted users, or the public.

Tips for success:

- Price smartly (not too high, not too free)

- Limit supply to increase perceived value
- Offer staggered access (e.g., whitelist, then public)

⚠ *Don't rely solely on this.* If this is your only revenue stream, you're building a "cash grab," not a business.

Revenue Stream #2: Royalties on Secondary Sales

NOW WE'RE TALKING **passive income.**

Every time someone resells your NFT on a marketplace like OpenSea, you earn a percentage (typically 5–10%).

Why it works:

It rewards long-term builders. The more people trade your NFT, the more you earn—without doing anything new.

Pro tip:

Use platforms or custom contracts that **enforce royalties**, as some marketplaces now bypass them.

Revenue Stream #3: Token-Gated Commerce

NFT = ACCESS.

You can link NFTs to:

- **Merch stores**
- **Event tickets**
- **Online courses or masterclasses**
- **Live podcast or webinar recordings**
- **Software subscriptions or tools**

Example: Hold a certain NFT = unlock a 30% lifetime discount or premium feature. Boom—loyalty meets revenue.

Revenue Stream #4: Events & IRL Experiences

WEB3 LOVES IRL NOW more than ever. You can monetize by hosting:

- NFT-only events or meetups
- Conferences, masterminds, or retreats
- Live art shows or gaming tournaments

Sell NFT passes or auction high-tier VIP experiences. This builds real community *and* income.

Revenue Stream #5: In-Game Economies

IF YOUR NFT IS PART of a game or metaverse, your economy can include:

- Land sales
- In-game item NFTs
- Upgrades and skins
- Power boosts, accessories, and XP tools

This model is HUGE in **play-to-earn** games like Axie Infinity or Sandbox. And yes—Chibi Dinos taps this model too.

Revenue Stream #6: Staking & Yield Mechanics

THIS IS FOR ADVANCED projects.

Staking lets users **lock their NFTs** to earn a utility token or rewards. Think of it like putting money in a bank and earning interest.

Your project can:

- Offer a governance token
- Create an internal economy
- Allow token-to-NFT upgrades or evolutions

⚠ *Make sure this is legally compliant in your country.*

Bonus: Brand Collaborations & Sponsorships

IF YOUR NFT PROJECT builds a recognizable brand, sponsors will come.

You can:

- Partner with streetwear or digital art brands
- Do sponsored airdrops or NFT collabs
- Co-host events or podcasts
- Feature sponsors in lore, visuals, or games

In the world of Sean Mike Kelly—this is how **influence meets innovation.**

Summary: Your NFT Empire Revenue

Checklist

PRIMARY SALES

Secondary Market Royalties

Token-Gated Access

Events & Experiences

Gaming Models

Staking & Tokens

Brand Partnerships

Remember: **Diverse income = sustainable success.**

In Web3, value doesn't just come from what you launch—it comes from what you build next.

— Sean Mike Kelly

Chapter 5: The Community Engine

How to Build & Scale Web3 Loyalty

In Web2, businesses were built around customers.

In Web3, businesses are built around **communities.**

If you look at any successful NFT project—whether it's Bored Ape Yacht Club, Chibi Dinos, or Pudgy Penguins—they didn't just sell tokens...

They built **tribes, movements**, and **loyal fanbases** who live, breathe, and rep their project 24/7.

I've seen this firsthand through my own launches and through *Digital Social Hour* guests who've built massive ecosystems. So in this chapter, I'm giving you the **exact playbook** for building community that lasts—**before, during, and after** your NFT mint.

Step 1: Define Your Community's Identity

ASK YOURSELF:

- Who are they?
- What do they care about?
- What do they stand for?
- What kind of culture are you creating?

Example:

Chibi Dinos wasn't just "basketball meets NFTs." It was a **Web3 sports league** where people picked teams, repped them like NBA fans, and got rewarded for their loyalty.

Give your community an identity they're proud to rep.

Step 2: Launch a Strong Discord or Telegram

DISCORD IS THE **heartbeat** of any NFT community.

Set up:

- Welcome channels
- Announcements
- Team intros
- Holder-only chats
- Fan art / memes
- Roles (OG, Whitelist, Mod, etc.)

Use bots like **Collab.Land** or **Dyno** to automate access and engagement.

⚠ Don't ghost your own server. Be active. Be real. Be present.

Step 3: Create Ongoing Value

AIRDROPS, PERKS, EVENTS, and alpha leaks are cool—but your real value comes from:

- Showing up daily
- Responding to holders
- Delivering on your roadmap

- Building things *with* the community (co-creation FTW)

Create:

- Weekly town halls
- Voting proposals (DAOs, governance, future drops)
- Behind-the-scenes dev or art streams
- Exclusive holder polls, merch, or events

The more they're involved, the more loyal they become.

Step 4: Use FOMO—But Ethically

YOU NEED MOMENTUM. So yes, use:

- Whitelists
- Time-based drops
- "Last chance" campaigns

But make sure they're backed by **value**, not just urgency.

Trust is your greatest asset. Break it once, and your project might not survive.

Step 5: Turn Holders into Ambassadors

WHEN YOUR HOLDERS FEEL valued, they turn into your **marketers**.

Encourage:

- Fan art contests

- Twitter raids
- Meme culture
- IRL meetups
- Referral rewards or ambassador programs

Every holder should feel like they *own a piece* of the empire—not just a token.

Step 6: Don't Just Build a Community—Build a Movement

THE MOST ICONIC WEB3 projects feel like movements. Your NFT isn't just a product—it's a symbol. A lifestyle. A digital badge of belonging.

The goal is to get people to say:

"I'm not just in the project. I *am* the project."

That's where loyalty turns into **legacy**.

Community Checklist

CLEAR IDENTITY & STORY

Strong communication channel (Discord, TG)
Constant value (airdrops, updates, BTS access)
FOMO mechanics (done right)
Empowered holders
Culture that grows beyond the token

You can clone art. You can fork code. But you can't copy a loyal community.

— *Sean Mike Kelly*

Chapter 6: Web3 Marketing

Hype, Influence & Scaling Your Message

You've built your NFT. The art is ◈. The utility is real. The roadmap? Solid.

But guess what?

None of it matters if no one knows you exist.

Web3 is crowded. Thousands of projects launch every week. If you want to stand out, you need more than a good idea—you need **masterful marketing.**

Here's the truth:

> You don't need millions of followers.
> You need the right people to **care** at the right time.

Let me show you how to make them care—Sean Mike Kelly style.

Step 1: Build In Public

WEB3 LOVES TRANSPARENCY. Start marketing **before you launch**—at least 60–90 days out.

Share:

- Behind-the-scenes of the art process
- Smart contract or dev logs

- AMA sessions or founder intros
- Sneak peeks of NFT traits or game mechanics

Twitter threads, Instagram reels, Discord updates—go all in. Let people feel like they're **part of the build**.

Step 2: Leverage Influencers (The Right Way)

WEB3 INFLUENCERS ARE powerful—but it's not just about big names.

Look for:

- NFT Twitter thought leaders (5K–100K followers)
- Discord mods and community leaders
- YouTubers or podcasters in your niche
- Niche meme accounts with cult followings

Tips:

- Give them free access, not just paid promos
- Let them co-host Twitter Spaces or IG Lives
- Share real utility—not just "mint soon" spam

Build relationships > Buy shoutouts.

Step 3: Twitter, Threads, & Spaces

TWITTER IS WEB3'S PLAYGROUND. Learn the game.

Post daily:

- Teasers and art previews
- Lore drops and storytelling threads
- Polls, giveaways, and whitelist contests
- Founder insights + hot takes

Host or join **Twitter Spaces** weekly—chop it up with other founders, influencers, or community voices.

◈ Tools:

- Tweet Hunter (for scheduling)
- Hypefury (for engagement boosts)
- Zealy (for gamified community engagement)

Step 4: Get Press (Even If You're New)

PRESS ADDS **credibility**. Even 2–3 good placements can legitimize your project.

Start with:

- Medium.com articles about your project
- Submitting to NFT-based platforms (like NFT Now, Decrypt, Cointelegraph)
- Podcast guest appearances

Create a simple **media kit**:

- Project summary
- Key art samples
- Team bios
- Contact info / whitelist page

Step 5: Run Hype Campaigns

WANT ATTENTION? GIVE people a reason to *show up*.

Try:

- Limited-time airdrops
- "Mint 3, get 1 free" bonuses
- Treasure hunts or lore puzzles
- NFT raffles for early supporters
- Surprise merch drops or WL contests

Use scarcity + rewards = dopamine magic ◈

Step 6: Deliver Real Value, Not Empty Promises

THE MARKET IS SMARTER now. It's seen rugs. It's seen hype cycles die.

To win, you need **trust + transparency**.

That means:

- Weekly project updates
- Being visible in Discord and socials
- Owning mistakes and showing progress
- Celebrating community wins (not just sales)

Because in Web3, **your brand is your word.**

Web3 Marketing Checklist

BUILD IN PUBLIC

Collaborate with real influencers
Dominate Twitter + Spaces
Get press and backlinks
Create viral campaigns
Prioritize value, not just volume

Good marketing fills a Discord. Great marketing builds a movement.
— Sean Mike Kelly

Chapter 7: Web3 Mistakes to Avoid

The NFT Founder Survival Guide

You've heard the hype.

"NFTs are the future."

"Community is everything."

"Mint out in 2 minutes or you're dead."

But here's the truth: most NFT projects fail—not because of bad art or lack of tech—but because of **avoidable founder mistakes.**

If you're serious about building something **long-term**, then read this chapter twice. It might save your project. Maybe even your reputation.

Let's break down the biggest mistakes I've seen—and yes, made myself—so you don't repeat them.

Mistake 1: Launching Too Fast

SPEED KILLS IN WEB3.

I get it—you're excited. The art is ready. The Discord's popping. But don't mint just because **others are**. Ask:

- Have you built enough trust?
- Does the market know your *why*?
- Is your utility clear?

- Is your team ready for chaos?

Rushing to mint often leads to botched launches, failed reveals, and burnt-out founders.

Take time to build buzz, educate your audience, and test everything (especially the contract).

Mistake 2: Overpromising Utility

"WE'RE BUILDING A GAME."

"You'll earn passive income."

"We have partnerships with Nike and Tesla." ⍰

Unless you have legal agreements, working MVPs, and funding, don't promise things you can't deliver.

You don't need 100 features. You need 1 **killer value prop** done right.

Underpromise. Overdeliver. Surprise your holders in the best way.

Mistake 3: Going Silent After the Mint

THIS ONE IS DEADLY.

Founders disappear after mint. The roadmap dies. The Discord fades. Community feels abandoned. And suddenly... "Is this a rug?"

Even if things go wrong—**communicate**.

- Weekly updates
- Founder voice notes or live calls
- Sneak peeks of development
- Acknowledging delays with transparency

Presence > perfection.

Mistake 4: Ignoring Community Feedback

YOU ARE *not* building alone. You're building with them.

Common sins:

- Ignoring holder suggestions
- Making major changes without input
- Banning critics instead of addressing concerns

Yes, you're the visionary. But your holders are investors, fans, and co-creators. Let them feel heard.

Set up structured channels (AMA, feedback forms, DAO votes).

Mistake 5: Prioritizing Hype Over Substance

TOO MANY PROJECTS SPEND 90% on launch... and nothing on delivery.

Flashy trailers, celeb shoutouts, Discord raids... but after mint? Silence. No updates. No utility. No roadmap follow-through.

And then the floor price crashes. Fast.

Hype is fuel—but your *product* is the engine. Without that, the car doesn't move.

Mistake 6: Weak Tokenomics & Royalties

POORLY THOUGHT-OUT royalty splits, inflationary tokens, or no long-term plan = disaster.

- Don't launch a token unless you know how it will create real value.
- Don't offer staking unless it's legal and sustainable.
- Don't rely only on royalties—markets change fast.

Study real projects with strong economies (like DeGods, Azuki, or Pudgy Penguins).

Mistake 7: Copy-Paste Projects

LAUNCHING A CLONE OF the last trending PFP won't cut it anymore.

If your project feels like:

- "X" but with a different animal
- No real backstory or mission
- AI-generated art with no soul

...it's already dead.

Be original. Or be meaningful. Or be both. But don't be lazy.

Red Flags for Founders to Watch

- No dev on the team
- Art outsourced to Fiverr with no licensing
- All hype, no roadmap

- Fake followers & bots
- "Team reveal coming after mint" ◈
- Floor-price obsession instead of brand vision

IF IT FEELS SHADY... it probably is.

> *The Web3 space doesn't forgive easily. But it respects those who show up, own up, and build up.*
>
> *— Sean Mike Kelly*

Your Survival Guide Recap:

LAUNCH SLOW. BUILD trust.
Promise only what you can deliver.
Stay present post-mint.
Listen to your holders.
Focus on value, not just vibes.
Design strong tokenomics.
Be original. Be real.

Chapter 8: Future-Proofing Your NFT Brand

Longevity in Web3

Web3 moves at breakneck speed.

What's hot today can be forgotten tomorrow. A top-trending NFT can go from a 10Ξ floor to meme status overnight. So the real question isn't *how to launch*. It's **how to last**.

In this chapter, we're shifting from hype to **legacy**—the long-term mindset that separates quick flips from cultural brands.

As someone who's witnessed the rise and fall of projects up close (and built brands that endured), let me show you how to create a project that doesn't just survive... but thrives for years.

1. Build With Pivot Power

DON'T FALL IN LOVE with the format. Fall in love with the **mission.**

Your PFP project may evolve into a:

- Web3 game
- Fashion brand
- DAO

- Educational platform
- Token-gated social club
- Virtual sports franchise (*Chibi Dinos*, anyone?)

Flexibility = survival.

Ask:

If NFTs stopped trending tomorrow, what would your brand *still* offer?

2. Define a Strong Brand DNA

LONG-LASTING PROJECTS have something deeper than traits and utility.

They have:

- A recognizable *visual language*
- A *voice* that resonates across content
- *Values* that hold the community together
- *Storylines* that evolve with time

Your NFT is the **entry point**—but your **brand is the world** they live in.

Think:

- Pudgy Penguins = positivity & empowerment
- Azuki = anime street culture
- DeGods = raw, rebellious energy
- YOU = ?

3. Expand into Physical & Lifestyle Products

WEB3 BRANDS ARE GOING IRL. And that's no accident.

Launch:

- Limited-edition merch
- Streetwear or collectibles
- Skate decks, plush toys, or premium cards
- Coffee table books or art prints
- Collaborations with real-world brands

This adds **tangible value**—and creates physical proof of culture.

Bonus: NFTs as claim passes for physical goods = utility with soul.

4. Enter the Gaming & Metaverse Arena

GAMING IS WHERE NFTS shine.

If your project has:

- Characters
- Items
- Lands
- Power-ups or stories

...you've got the potential to evolve into a full-blown **Web3 game or metaverse experience**.

Look at what Yuga Labs is doing with Otherside. You don't need their budget—you need vision + execution.

Use platforms like:

- Unreal Engine / Unity
- The Sandbox / Decentraland
- OnCyber or Spatial

5. Community-Governed Scaling (DAOs & Voting)

THE FUTURE OF BRANDS = **co-ownership**.

Turn your holders into decision-makers by:

- Proposing product ideas
- Voting on future collabs
- Choosing artists, devs, or themes
- Participating in profit-sharing models

DAOs are complex, but when done right? They create brands no single founder could've imagined alone.

Tools: Snapshot, Aragon, Tally

6. Stay Data-Driven & Community-First

USE TOOLS TO TRACK:

- Holder activity
- Retention over time
- Mint participation
- Wallet loyalty
- Floor price + volume + sentiment trends

More importantly, **ask your community**:

- "What should we build next?"
- "What's missing?"
- "How do we make this better?"

Your biggest asset isn't your smart contract—it's your believers.

7. Evolve Without Losing the Soul

YOU CAN REBRAND. PIVOT. Merge. Airdrop. Burn. Stake.

But don't lose the **why**.

Every long-term brand has changed form—just not its **purpose**.

Your NFT isn't the final product—it's the **entry point to an evolving experience**. So keep adapting, but stay rooted.

> *Consistency of soul beats consistency of strategy.*
> *— Sean Mike Kelly*

Future-Proofing Playbook:

STAY ADAPTABLE (PIVOT-ready)

Build beyond NFTs (games, products, brands)

Cement your brand DNA

Explore IRL, gaming, DAO, merch

Keep community in the driver's seat

Think in decades, not drops

Chapter 9: Case Studies

NFT Brands That Did It Right

Thousands of NFT projects have launched.

Very few became **brands**.

Fewer still became **movements**.

And almost none became **empires**.

The ones that did?

They didn't just mint out. They built worlds, economies, identities.

In this chapter, I'll break down some of the most iconic Web3 projects—and show you what you can learn from them.

1. Pudgy Penguins: From Meme to Merch Empire

LAUNCHED: July 2021

Founder (current): Luca Netz

Initial Vibe: Cute PFPs with meme potential

What Went Right:

- **Community Takeover** — After initial mismanagement, the community forced a leadership change. Enter Luca Netz: a brand visionary.
- **IP Expansion** — Toys in Walmart. Storybooks.

Licensing deals.

- **Brand DNA:** Positivity, wholesomeness, community-first.
- **Platform Play:** Launched **Pudgy World**, a digital universe bridging Web2 and Web3.

Key Takeaway:

→ You can revive a project with *vision* and *execution*. The IP is the asset. Build beyond OpenSea.

2. Azuki: Anime Culture + Web3 Cool

LAUNCHED: Jan 2022

Creator: Chiru Labs

What Went Right:

- **Insane Art Direction** — Clean, crisp anime aesthetic that screamed brand potential.
- **Lore + Universe** — Not just NFTs, but a world. Characters. Storylines.
- **Beanz + Physical Drops** — Follow-up collections. Streetwear. Event presence.
- **The Spirit DAO** — Created culture through storytelling and exclusivity.

Challenges:

Controversy over the founder's past "rug" projects.

Recovery:

Strong branding, transparent comms, and consistent value.

Key Takeaway:

→ Vision, community storytelling, and aesthetic unity make people *feel* part of something bigger.

3. VeeFriends: The Power of Personal Brand

LAUNCHED: May 2021

Creator: Gary Vaynerchuk

What Went Right:

- **Web2 Leverage:** Gary Vee used his 10+ years of content, audience, and trust to launch strong.
- **Utility-Driven:** NFTs granted access to **VeeCon**, mentorships, events.
- **IRL Integration:** Toys, books, partnerships with Mattel and Macy's.

What Made It Work:

He didn't launch art. He launched **a value-packed community pass** backed by trust.

Key Takeaway:

→ If you're a creator with audience and credibility, NFTs are your **ownership rails.**

4. Bored Ape Yacht Club: The Cultural Takeover

LAUNCHED: April 2021

Creator: Yuga Labs

What Went Right:

- **Exclusive Identity:** "You're not just buying art. You're joining a club."
- **Celeb Endorsements:** Snoop, Eminem, Neymar, Jimmy Fallon.
- **Mutants + Kennel Club + Otherside:** Built a *multi-IP ecosystem.*
- **DAO, Token, and Metaverse** — Pushed the boundaries of NFT evolution.

What Made It Explode:

Perfect mix of meme, utility, exclusivity, and vibes.

Key Takeaway:

→ Culture + timing + narrative = rocket fuel. BAYC didn't chase virality. They created it.

5. Chibi Dinos: The Sports Franchise Vision (Sean Mike Kelly)

LAUNCHED: 2021

Creator: Sean Mike Kelly

What Went Right:

- **Fusion of Sports + NFTs** — Unique concept: basketball-playing dinosaur characters.
- **Web3 Franchise Model:** Each NFT belonged to a team; fans followed, repped, and played along.
- **Merch + Lore + Gameplay:** Bridged entertainment, sports culture, and NFTs.
- **Vision Beyond PFPs:** Kelly aimed to build an entertainment *empire*, not just a collectible.

What's Smart:

Entertainment + sports + NFTs = *huge audience potential*

Key Takeaway:

→ Niche + clear narrative + gamified utility = sticky brand. Create worlds, not just wallets.

Common Threads Across the Winners:

Winning Factor	Why It Matters
Strong Community	Creates loyalty beyond market cycles
Utility & Access	Gives NFTs real-world relevance
IP & Merch Potential	Expands audience + revenue
Leadership Transparency	Builds trust in tough times
Storytelling & Lore	Emotional connection = retention
Culture Creation	You don't just hold the NFT—you rep it

A floor price is not a brand. A Twitter following is not a community. Real brands live in the hearts of the people.

— Sean Mike Kelly

Chapter 10: Your Empire Launch Plan

From Idea to Mint to Momentum

You've got the vision.

You've studied the best.

You've learned the strategy, the story, the tech, and the traps.

Now it's time to **launch**.

This chapter gives you a full **A-to-Z roadmap** for launching an NFT project that doesn't just mint out—but leaves a legacy.

Step 1: Craft a Clear Concept

BEFORE YOU BUILD A Discord, design a trait, or tweet your first sneak peek... lock in your **mission**:

- What problem are you solving?
- What culture are you creating?
- Why should people *care*?

Define:

- Theme (what it looks/feels like)
- Utility (what holders *get*)
- Vision (where it's going)

Clarity upfront = stronger marketing + stronger community.

Step 2: Design Your NFT Collection

DON'T OVERCOMPLICATE. Start simple, but meaningful.

Choose:

- Total supply (100 to 10,000+)
- Number of traits + rarity structure
- 1/1s, animated pieces, or generative collections
- Art style (hand-drawn, AI-assisted, pixel, 3D, etc.)

Pro tips:

- Hire artists with a long-term vision, not just quick gigs.
- Create a consistent visual identity across your website, social media, and NFTs.

Step 3: Assemble the Dream Team

YOU DON'T NEED 20 PEOPLE—BUT you need **the right people**:

Role	Why It's Crucial
Dev (Solidity etc.)	For smart contract + mint logic
Artist/Designer	For visuals, brand, website
Community Manager	For Discord, holders, vibes
Marketer/Storyteller	For Twitter, press, threads

Even if you start lean—wear hats, but plan to scale.

Step 4: Build the Infrastructure

SMART CONTRACT

Website + Mint Page

Discord Server (fully structured)

Twitter + other socials

Community onboarding flows

Collab tools (Zealy, Premint, Collab.Land)

Use testnets before mainnet launch.

And yes—**audits matter**. Don't risk holders' wallets.

Step 5: Execute a Pre-Mint Hype Campaign

TIMEFRAME: 30–60 days before mint

Main goals: Community, buzz, education

Your toolkit:

- Twitter threads + Spaces
- Giveaways + WL contests
- Influencer collabs + AMA circuits
- Partner drops with other NFT brands
- Medium blogs + storytelling

Build **value before volume**. Hype only works if people *trust* you.

Step 6: Launch with Clarity

MINT DAY CHECKLIST:

- Stress-test everything beforehand
- Go live with founders visible
- Discord voice + Twitter Space live during launch
- Post clear instructions with wallet safety tips
- Have mods on high alert for scams

Optional:

- Tiered mint (OG > WL > Public)
- Reveal schedule (instantly or delayed)

Post-mint? Celebrate... but then **keep building.**

Step 7: Sustain Momentum Post-Mint

THIS IS WHERE MOST projects fail. Not you.

Your playbook:

- Weekly updates (even small wins)
- Deliver utilities in sprints (don't wait 6 months)
- Airdrop surprises + WL for next phases
- Launch merch, lore, staking, or token-gated tools
- Get community *involved* in future decisions

Consistency = trust. Trust = longevity.

Step 8: Expand Into Empire Mode

AFTER MINT, EXPLORE:

- IRL events

- Token economy
- Partnerships with brands
- Expansion collections
- DAO-based governance
- Game or metaverse integrations
- Brand licensing and IP deals

You don't need to rush. But you do need to **scale with purpose**.

Empire Builder's Bonus: Sean Mike Kelly's Launch Laws

1. **Start with why**
2. **Build in public**
3. **Let community co-create**
4. **Underpromise, overdeliver**
5. **Think like a brand, not a drop**
6. **Stay visible—every damn day**
7. **Measure what matters: trust > floor**
8. **Legacy over loudness**

Final Word

THIS ISN'T THE END. It's the **beginning**.

You're not just creating NFTs.

You're building an **empire of value, vision, and vibes**.

Keep showing up. Keep listening. Keep evolving.

Because in Web3, **fortune favors the doers**—not just the dreamers.

One NFT drop can change your life. But one consistent mission can change the world.

— Sean Mike Kelly

NFT Empire: You're Ready to Launch

YOU NOW HAVE:

- The strategy
- The blueprint
- The mindset
- The edge

Go build. Go lead. Go disrupt.
Your empire awaits.

...The End...

About the Author

Sean Mike Kelly (born February 14, 1997) is an American entrepreneur, podcast host, and founder of Jersey Champs. He gained recognition for building one of the top custom jersey brands online and later launched the *Digital Social Hour* podcast. Kelly has also been active in e-commerce, NFTs, and digital media.

Read more at https://seankelly.io/.